PROMISE KIDS ON THE PROMISE PATH

LEARNING HOW TO FOLLOW GOD'S DIRECTIONS

THIS WAY TO PROMISE PATH

BY LINDA M. WASHINGTON

Illustrated by Anita Duffala

MW01106757

Promise Kids Prayer

Dear Jesus,

I want to live like a Promise Kid by following your directions.
But sometimes I don't know what to do. Teach me how to follow you.
Help me _____ (name something for which you
need God's help). In your name,

Amen.

Cover Illustration and Design: De Leon Design
Editors: Debbie Bible, Marian Oliver
Text Illustrations: Anita Duffala

© 1999 Mainstay Church Resources
Published by Mainstay Church Resources
Printed in the United States of America
ISBN 1-57849-108-8

All rights reserved. No portion of this book may be reproduced in any form or by any means—electronic or mechanical, including photocopying, recording, or information storage and retrieval systems—without written permission of Mainstay Church Resources, Box 30, Wheaton, IL 60189-0030, (630) 668-7292.

Mainstay Church Resources' passion is to facilitate revival among God's people by helping pastors help them develop healthy spiritual habits in nine vital areas that always characterize genuine times of spiritual awakening. To support this goal, Mainstay Church Resources uses a C.H.U.R.C.H. strategy to provide practical tools and resources, including the annual 50-Day Spiritual Adventure, the Seasonal Advent Celebration, the 4-Week Festival of Worship, and the Pastor's Toolbox.

All Scriptures, unless otherwise indicated, are taken from the International Children's Bible, New Century Version, copyright © 1983, 1986, 1988 by Word Publishing, Dallas, Texas 75039. Used by permission.

Scripture quotations marked (NIV) are taken from the HOLY BIBLE, NEW INTERNATIONAL VERSION®. Copyright © 1973, 1978, 1984 by International Bible Society. Used by permission of Zondervan Publishing House. All rights reserved.

"Accelerated spiritual growth
for individuals and families"

MAINSTAY
Church Resources

Helping Pastors
Help People Grow

To Kids (and Parents)!

Hey Kids!

When Australians take a long journey, they call it "going on a walk-about." For this 50-Day Spiritual Adventure, you'll go on a walkabout too, a walkabout along the Promise Path. This is the path you'll travel to discover eight different ways you can be a Promise Kid. A Promise Kid is someone who loves Jesus and wants to do what he would do. On this Adventure you'll learn how to follow God's directions at home, at church, at school, and in your neighborhood. And the best part is, you don't have to walk the Promise Path alone. Jesus has promised to be with you to help you live like a Promise Kid.

On page 14 there's a neat T-shirt decal you can trace to make a special shirt to wear on your Adventure. But be sure you read the directions carefully before starting. And you may need the help of an adult.

To stay fit for the journey, you'll need to pay attention to five Path Keeper Skills. These skills will help you grow closer to Jesus and other important people in your life. They will also give you support when you need help. So, the sooner you get started, the better! Are you ready? Then put on your walking shoes. Let's go!

PATH KEEPER SKILL 1
Make memories with Jesus.

PATH KEEPER SKILL 2
Find a Promise Path partner.

PATH KEEPER SKILL 3
Clear your path with PURITY.

PATH KEEPER SKILL 4
Care for those you care about.

PATH KEEPER SKILL 5
Get to know different kinds of people on your path.

Get Ready for the Journey!

If you're going on a journey, you need to know two things: where you're starting from and where you'll end up. You're about to begin a 50-Day Adventure to learn how to follow God's directions. Each week of the Adventure has a direction that will guide you along the Promise Path. Here are the directions you'll find.

Promise Kids:

Week 1—Stop and think about Jesus

Week 2—Find friends who help them follow Jesus

Week 3—Do what Jesus would do

Week 4—Make family time important

Week 5—Get involved at church

Week 6—Accept others as Jesus does

Week 7—Make a difference in their world

Week 8—Stay on the Promise Path

YOU ARE HERE

How to Use Your Journal

THE PATH OF A PROMISE KID

Take a quick walk through the journal. As you begin the Adventure, there are two warm-up days to help you get to know, and get excited about, the Adventure. There is one journal page for each day of the week, except for Saturday and Sunday. Usually those days will be combined into one weekend page. Each activity page has the following four sections:

1. WORD WALK
Each day you'll walk through the Word (the Bible) with a different Scripture passage to look up and read. The passages will help you understand what Bible-time people learned about God's directions.

2. CHECK POINT
Runners receive water and encouragement at check points. In this journal, this is the place where you'll find information to help you understand the Word Walk passage. Often there will be

questions to guide you. You can write your answers or talk them over with a parent. You might even use pictures or symbols in your answers. Do what helps you learn best.

3. STRENGTH BUILDER
To keep up your spiritual strength, you'll find an activity each day to help you put what you've read into practice.

4. SKILL PRACTICE
This is a short list of ways to practice the five Path Keeper Skills described on pages 8–12. These skills are an important part of your Adventure. You will also be reminded to learn the Path Lighter Memory Verses each week. For a complete list of the memory verses, turn to the next page.

Path Lighter Memory Verses

The Bible describes God's Word as a light for our path (Psalm 119:105). The eight memory passages of this Adventure will help make clear the way along the Promise Path. They are printed here for your convenience. They come from the International Children's Bible, but you may choose to use another version of the Bible if you prefer.

Week 1
God says, "Be quiet and know that I am God. I will be supreme over all the nations. I will be supreme in the earth."
Psalm 46:10

WEEK 2
A good person takes advice from his friends. But an evil person is easily led to do wrong.
Proverbs 12:26

Week 3
Let us run the race that is before us and never give up. We should remove from our lives anything that would get in the way. And we should remove the sin that so easily catches us. Let us look only to Jesus.
Hebrews 12:1–2

Week 4
"Honor your father and mother." This is the first commandment that has a promise with it. The promise is: "Then everything will be well with you."
Ephesians 6:2–3

Week 5
You should not stay away from the church meetings, as some are doing. But you should meet together and encourage each other.
Hebrews 10:25

Week 6
God does not see the same way people see. People look at the outside of a person, but the Lord looks at the heart.
1 Samuel 16:7

Week 7
You should be a light for other people. Live so that they will see the good things you do. Live so that they will praise your Father in heaven.
Matthew 5:16

Week 8
You will teach me God's way to live. Being with you will fill me with joy. At your right hand I will find pleasure forever.
Psalm 16:11

Be a Word-class Traveler!

World-class travelers take time to study maps of places to which they travel. This helps them avoid getting lost during a journey. Say . . . you look like a world-class traveler. But for this journey, I think a more accurate description would be a "Word-class" traveler. During this Adventure, the Bible will be your map for the Promise Path. You'll need to spend some time in the Word every day in different Word Walk passages and with the Path Lighter Memory Verses. Use the following "rules of the road" as you navigate through the Word. Or, come up with your own "rules."

• Make sure you have a Bible that's easy for you to understand.
• Your Bible's table of contents is your best friend if you're not sure of the location of a Bible book. But

if you really want to be a "Word-class" traveler, take the time to learn the order of the books of the Bible. This is a skill you can use for life!
• At the beginning of each week you can use sticky notes to mark the location of each daily Word Walk scripture passage. If you mark all of the locations beforehand, you'll have more time to spend in your journal.

As a "Word-class" traveler on the Promise Path, there are five skills you need to know. These five skills will help you along the road to learning God's directions. Each one will be described on its own page.

Path Keeper Skill 1:
Make memories with Jesus

Marathon runners need the help of an encouraging coach to work on their pace. If they run too fast, they tire out before the end of the race. If they run too slow . . . well, you get the idea. Many marathon runners often say they don't remember much of what went on during the race. But they do remember the meaningful times they spent with their coaches.

Being a Promise Kid means you're on a Promise Path, a path to help you follow God's directions. Promise Kids need to spend time with the ultimate coach: Jesus. Spending time with Jesus helps create memories you can take with you forever, like the memories you have from special times with your family and friends.

You can spend time with Jesus by reading your Bible and praying each day. This journal will give you other ideas to help you stop and think about him every day.

Practicing the 5 Path Keeper Skills

Taking a trip is always more fun when you have a friend along. But suppose you and your friend couldn't agree on where you were going or how you would get there? That would make the trip difficult, wouldn't it?

Promise Kids who want to follow God's directions need others in their lives who want to help them do just that. This skill encourages you to find a friend who will help you follow God. Each week throughout the Adventure you can share with that friend what you're learning. And while you're at it, why not ask your partner to pray for you? If your friend's on the Adventure too, you can help each other.

You'll focus on this skill during Week 2.

Path Keeper Skill 3:
Clear Your Path with PURITY

Promise Kids want to follow God's directions. But all of us mess up sometimes. When we do, we need to ask God for forgiveness and for help to do things right. Clearing your path with PURITY can help get rid of the stuff that tries to keep you from following God. Purity means loving God and making good choices. Each letter in the word PURITY shows something you can do regularly to be pure.

Put away put-downs: This helps us identify the bad things we say that hurt others. It also helps us put away other wrong things in our lives.

Undo unkind actions: This helps us make things right with the people we've hurt.

Run from things you know are wrong: This reminds us to run from the temptations in our lives toward the God who helps us.

Invite an adult who loves you to help you: This reminds us that we don't have to do everything alone. A loving adult in your life can be there to pray with you and help you when you're feeling tempted to do wrong.

Think God's thoughts: This reminds you to think *What would Jesus do?* in the situation you find most tempting. Then do what he would do, or what he would want you to do.

Yell for joy (and high-five): This reminds us to celebrate when we triumph over temptation!

This skill goes with the topic for Week 3, which is "Do what Jesus would do." Jesus led a pure life. And you'll learn more about this skill during Week 3.

Practicing the 5 Path Keeper Skills

All of us have families. Those of us in God's family have two: the family we live with and our church family. As much as we love our families, sometimes we don't spend enough time with them or help to meet their needs. God wants his Promise Kids to spend time with and serve both their families. Here are some suggested ways to do this:

My Family Builders: These are daily ways to serve your family members. For example, you can make your parents' bed, slip an "I Love You" note to your sister or brother, volunteer for a chore that you don't usually do, thank your mom or dad for all they do for you, or give a word of encouragement to someone. You can also help plan fun activities to do with your family once every week or two. For example, you could go to a restaurant you've always wanted to try, take a long walk in the park together, or plan a family picnic.

God's Family Builders: These are ways you can serve the people in your church family. For example, you might pray for your Sunday school teacher or pastor. Call someone to encourage him or her during the week. Or, you might pick up a bulletin to send to an elderly person who can't attend church. You'll work on God's Family Builders in Week 5.

You can keep track of the Family Builders ideas you do each day by filling in the Family Builder Adventure Log on pages 32–33. Remember, the goal is to do My Family Builders each day of the Adventure. But you will be instructed about God's Family Builders in Week 5.

Path Keeper Skill 5:
Get to know different kinds of people on your path

There's a whole world out there, a world filled with many different kinds of people. Have you ever wondered about someone who is different from you? It's easy to fear or mistrust people you don't know much about. That's why this step encourages you to learn about people of other races or from other cultures. There are many different things you can do.

With your family, you might see a movie like *Ruby Bridges*. This is the true story of a young African-American girl who was the first of her race to go to a certain school. *The Girl Who Spelled Freedom* is about how an Asian family adjusts to life in America. *Night John* is the story of a former African-American slave who risked his life to help other African-American slaves learn how to read. Be sure to talk about the movies afterward. To learn more about people from other countries, you might go for a family meal at an ethnic restaurant. Or, take a trip to the library to find books about people from different cultures. Try learning a few words of their language. You could also use the Internet to find out about people from a different culture. If there are people of different cultures within your congregation, your family might invite that family over for a meal.

You'll learn more about this skill during Week 6.

GLOBAL VILLAGE

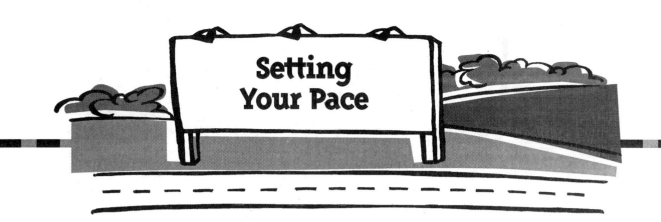

Setting Your Pace

IT'S ABOUT TIME

Choose a time each day to work in your journal when you won't be distracted. Plan on about 10–15 minutes to complete each journal page. Being a Promise Kid on the 50-Day Spiritual Adventure takes commitment. It's a promise you make to yourself and to God to keep your daily "appointment." But if you're like many kids today, you have a lot going on in your life. If you get so busy that you have to skip a page, don't worry! Just move on to the next exciting day. To help you keep track of the days you complete, use the Family Adventure Log on pages 32–33.

IT'S ABOUT PLACE

Choose a favorite spot where you can work on the Adventure. If you like being outside, grab your Bible and journal and head out. If indoors suits you better, make it your mission to find the best place to be quiet and concentrate.

Use the pocket organizer below to fill in the time and place you've chosen to work on your journal. Think about setting a goal for yourself for this Adventure. You might set an overall goal or a goal for each week of how many journal pages you will complete.

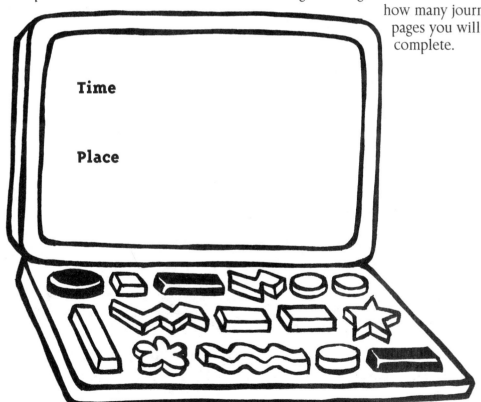

Time

Place

Promise Kids Decal

A Promise Kid needs to look the part. Use the T-shirt decal below to show the world that you are a Promise Kid: one who follows God's directions. Or, you might use it in another creative way: as part of a book cover or enlarged on a photocopier as a poster to hang in your room.

Promise Kids Decal

What you'll need:
- T-shirt (pre-washed)
- Pattern tracing-paper (from a fabric store)
- Fabric pens (from a crafts store)
- Pen or pencil

1. Place a piece of cardboard inside your T-shirt.
2. Place a piece of pattern-tracing paper colored-side down on the front of your T-shirt.
3. Make a copy of the Promise Kids Decal. Place the picture over the T-shirt. Trace it with a pen or pencil.
4. Use fabric pens to trace your outline on the T-shirt.

Some computer programs allow you to print T-shirt transfers. If you have access to a computer and scanner, you can scan the picture of the decal. Check the software's directions to see if you're allowed to use pictures other than the ones given in the program. The software kits usually come with transfer paper. Once printed, the picture has to be ironed onto the T-shirt.

Promise Kids on the Promise Path

THIS WAY TO PROMISE PATH

Friday

Warm Up

WORD WALK
Read 2 Peter 1:3–7.

CHECK POINT
This passage comes from a letter written by Peter, one of Jesus' disciples. His letter has helpful advice for Promise Kids on the Promise Path. Answer the questions to remind yourself of his advice.

1. What does God want us to do? (2 Peter 1:3)

2. Jesus has given us everything we need to live a godly life. Write three words that describe how that makes you feel.

3. Peter mentions that we've been given promises. Name a promise you've read about in the Bible. Why is it important to remember God's promises?

STRENGTH BUILDER
Everyone loves to receive gifts. And God loves to give them. Peter mentioned these eight gifts that God wants to add to our lives: faith, godliness, goodness, knowledge, self-control, kindness, love, and perseverance. Using the names of the gifts, write your own song to remember them. Using a familiar tune might be helpful.

SKILL PRACTICE
• Check out the Promise Kids Prayer on page 2.
• Begin thinking about Family Builders, ways you can serve your family members. You'll start keeping track of these on the first day of the Adventure. For more information on Family Builders, see page 11.

THIS WAY TO **PROMISE PATH**

Saturday

Warm Up

Gazette

WANT ADS

Wanted: A Friend
Description Below:

STRENGTH BUILDER

Friends enjoy spending time with each other. As an official friend of Jesus (FOJ), what will you do this coming week to spend time with him? Check one on the computer screen below.

SKILL PRACTICE

• Read the Promise Kids Prayer on page 2.
• Keep thinking about Family Builders, ways you can serve your family members. For more information on Family Builders, see page 11.

WORD WALK

Read John 15:9–14.

CHECK POINT

Jesus wanted his disciples to know how important friendship was to him. What does Jesus look for in a friend? Based on what you read in the passage, complete the ad above. Be sure to include the qualities Jesus looks for. Then think about these questions: Why are these qualities important? Do you fit the description?

❑ Pray.

❑ Read the Bible or a Christian book.

❑ Take a walk or skate and thank him for something he has created.

❑ Listen to a Christian cassette or CD.

❑ Other (Specify: _____).

WORD WALK
Read Luke 10:38–42.

CHECK POINT
Busy! Busy! Busy! That was Martha. She hardly had time to spend with her friend Jesus. Check out the Stress-o-Matic at the bottom of the page. This handy-dandy machine measures how worried or stressed a person might be. Use an X to show how you would rate Martha and Mary, then answer these questions:

1. What had Mary chosen to do? (Luke 10:39)

2. What was Jesus' advice for Martha? (10:42) (Use your own words.)

STRENGTH BUILDER
Now, take a breather on the Promise Path to think about your day. Rate yourself on the "Stress-o-Matic." How did you do? Have you done what you checked on yesterday's page for how you would spend time with Jesus?

SKILL PRACTICE
• Read the Promise Kids Prayer. Then close your eyes and think about Jesus for a few moments. What do you know to be true about him?
• Check out this week's Path Lighter Verse, Psalm 46:10, on page 6.
• Keep track of the Family Builders you try, using the list on pages 32–33. For more information on this, see page 11.

STRESS-O-MATIC

	Calm	A Little Worried	Majorly Stressed
Martha			
Mary			
Me			

THIS WAY TO PROMISE PATH

DAY 2

Monday

WORD WALK
Read Psalm 63:1–6.

CHECK POINT
David wrote this psalm to show how he felt about God. In the thought balloon below, write some of the phrases that describe how David felt about God. Put a star beside the one that best describes how you feel about God. Then, write two phrases that tell what David did to show how he felt about God. Draw a smiley face beside the one you will do today.

STRENGTH BUILDER
The Path Lighter Memory Verse for this week comes from a different psalm. It will remind you to stop and think about Jesus. You will need to hold it up to a mirror to figure out what it says.

God says, "Be quiet and know that I am God. I will be supreme over all the nations. I will be supreme in the earth." Psalm 46:10

SKILL PRACTICE
• Use the Promise Kids Prayer as you stop and think about Jesus today.
• Record your Family Builders on the list on pages 32–33. For more information on Family Builders, see page 11.

What David felt:

What David did:

DAY 3

THIS WAY TO **PROMISE PATH**

Tuesday

WORD WALK
Read Revelation 2:1–4.

CHECK POINT
The apostle John was one of Jesus' closest friends when Jesus was on earth. (An apostle is someone "sent out" to start churches.) One day, when John was stranded on an island, he saw the risen Jesus. Jesus gave John a message for the church in Ephesus. Ephesus was a large city in Asia Minor. (Ephesus is in the country of Turkey.) Like many messages, however, there was a good news part and a bad news part. What good things did Jesus say about the church? What was the bad news? Write your answers below.

Good News
(Revelation 2:2–3)

Bad News
(2:4)

- *(4 stomps or claps)* He's my best friend
- *(3 stomps or claps)* We're getting close
- *(2 stomps or claps)* I sort of know him
- *(1 stomp or clap)* Jesus who?

SKILL PRACTICE
- Read the Promise Kids Prayer on page 2. As you fill in the blank, think about what you need God to help you do to strengthen your love for Jesus.
- Learn Psalm 46:10. You might want to make up motions for the words. Learning the verse is a good way to stop and think about Jesus.
- Don't forget your Family Builder for today.

STRENGTH BUILDER
Well, it is time to stop and do a strength check. Let's see how strong your feelings are toward Jesus. Stomp the number of times indicated to show how you feel about Jesus today. Clap the number of times indicated to show how you would like to feel about Jesus:

THIS WAY TO **PROMISE PATH**

Wednesday

DAY 4

WORD WALK
Read 1 John 1:5–10.

CHECK POINT
Remember John, the writer of yesterday's Word Walk? He wrote the letter that today's passage comes from. He also wrote the Gospel of John, the three letters named for him, and Revelation. Use your Bible to answer the questions.

1. What is John's message? (1 John 1:5)

2. What do you think light means in this passage?

3. What is the darkness that keeps us from God? (If you're not sure, talk these last two questions over with a parent or another Christian adult.)

STRENGTH BUILDER
Speaking of light and dark, you'll need both to read the following message from 1 John 1:9. Shade in the shapes. When we walk in darkness, we need to do this to come back into God's light.

[CONFESS]

OUR SINS

SKILL PRACTICE
• If there is something you need to make right with God, why not take the time now to pray about it?
• Keep working at committing Psalm 46:10 to memory.
• What Family Builder will you do today? Record it on page 32.

ANSWER: CONFESS OUR SINS

WORD WALK
Read Mark 1:32, 35–39.

CHECK POINT
A car can't get very far without fuel. And neither can you. You need to eat good foods to keep up your strength, right? And this is especially true when you're busy. But you also need spiritual energy. For spiritual energy, you need the right "fuel." Even Jesus, after a busy day, needed to refuel. How did Jesus "refuel" himself? (Mark 1:35)

body to form each letter of PRAYER as you say it. Then read what you wrote. This is a great Family Builder. If you do it, be sure to record it on pages 32–33.

SKILL PRACTICE
• Pray the Promise Kids Prayer. Working on this journal page is a good way to stop and think about Jesus.
• Mark where you are in the Adventure by using the chart on pages 32–33.

STRENGTH BUILDER
If Jesus needed to refuel, then you do too. Use the letters in the word "prayer" to help you talk to God. For each letter in the picture to the right, write or say a need or something about him you appreciate. For example: "I need Peace" or "You are Perfect."

If you want to tell your family your acrostic during a family time, try using your

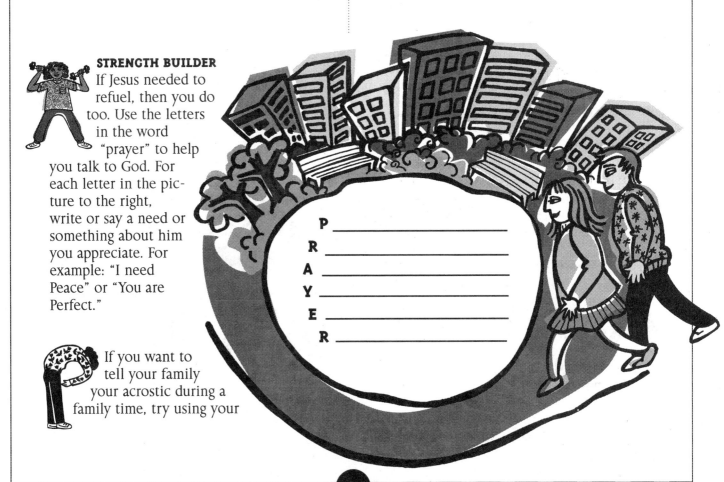

P _____

R _____

A _____

Y _____

E _____

R _____

THIS WAY TO **PROMISE PATH**

Friday

DAY 6

WORD WALK
Read Psalm 73:25–28.

CHECK POINT
Ever been on a trip so wonderful, you couldn't wait to tell others about it? You probably bought souvenirs to remember the journey. Today's Word Walk takes us on a trip back to Psalm Country. Yeeha! The psalm writers used their psalms to tell God how they felt about him.

One thing you probably noticed about the psalm is that the writer loved to spend time with God. But sometimes there are things that tempt us not to spend time with him. Put an X on the one item (in the circle) that most tempts you away from spending time with God. If you don't see what tempts you the most, write or draw it in the other circle.

STRENGTH BUILDER
You've come to the end of the first week of the Adventure. Review the journey so far. Which Word Walk do you remember the most? Why? Working in your journal has been a good way to make memories with Jesus and think about him this week.

SKILL PRACTICE
• Pray the Promise Kids Prayer on page 2. In the blank, ask God to help you resist the temptation you noted in "Strength Builder."
• Keep at those Family Builders. Use the list on pages 32–33 to record your acts of service.
• Have you learned Psalm 46:10? Did you use motions?

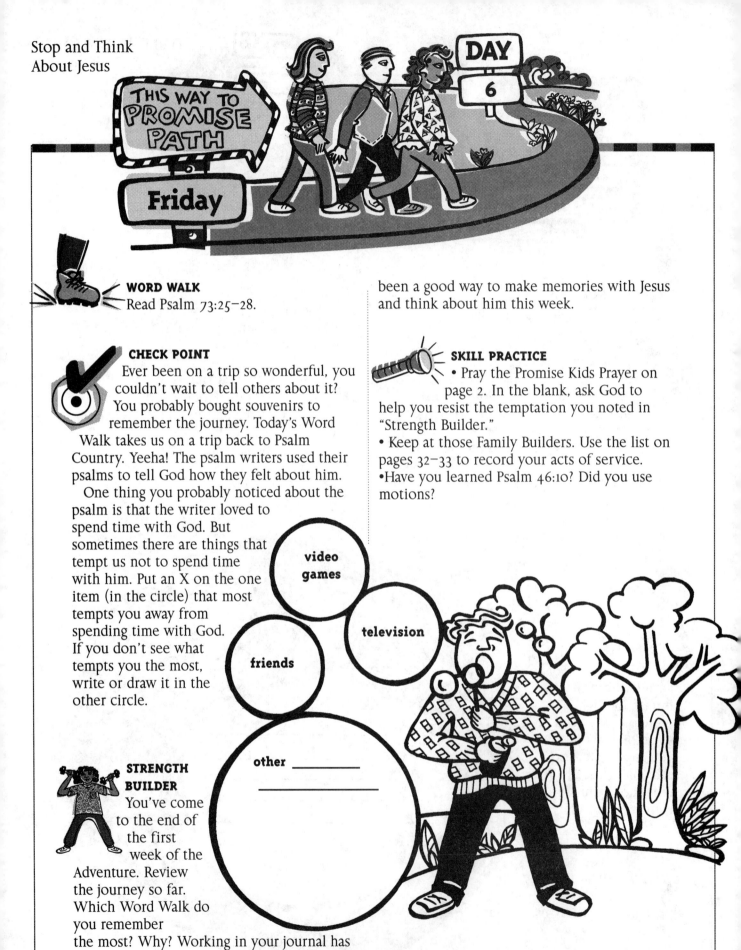

video games

television

friends

other _____
_____

THIS WAY TO PROMISE PATH

Sat/Sun

DAYS 7/8

WORD WALK
Read Proverbs 27:6, 9, 17.

CHECK POINT
Welcome to the Friendship Fork along the Promise Path. Throughout this week, we'll talk about—you guessed it—friendship. Today's Word Walk can help you understand what real friendship is. Look at the maze. Which way is the Proverbs 27 way to real friendship? Trace it with a pencil or crayon.

SKILL PRACTICE
• Use the Promise Kids Prayer on page 2 as a prayer to ask God to help you be a Proverbs kind of friend.
• Check out this week's Path Lighter Memory Verse, which is also from Proverbs—Proverbs 12:26. You can find a complete listing of the verses on page 6.
• Make plans to meet with a friend you trust and talk about the Adventure.

START

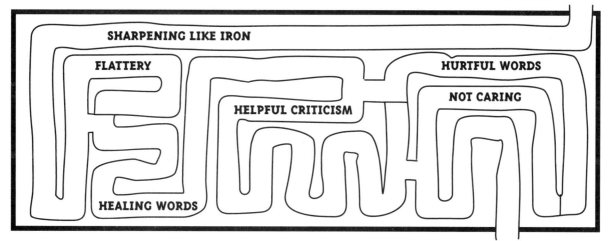

SHARPENING LIKE IRON

FLATTERY

HURTFUL WORDS

NOT CARING

HELPFUL CRITICISM

HEALING WORDS

STRENGTH BUILDER
Good friends are great to have. A good friend who wants to help you follow God is even better. Who can you count on in your life to encourage you to follow God? Write your friend's name at the end of the maze. Then take time to thank God for this Promise Path partner.

THIS WAY TO
PROMISE
PATH

Monday

DAY
9

WORD WALK
Read Romans 1:11–12.

CHECK POINT
Paul was a missionary who wrote most of the New Testament in his spare time. In today's Word Walk, Paul had some gifts for his friends in the church in Rome. Unscramble the words in the picture below to find what Paul wanted to give.

The first gift is a gift that keeps on giving. God gives each Christian this kind of gift. You'll learn more about this gift during Week 5.

Now, take a look at Paul's second gift. How can you use the gifts God gave you to do this for a friend?

SKILL PRACTICE
• During your prayer time, pray for a friend who needs encouragement. Ask God to show you what you can do to be a friend like Paul.
• If you made plans to meet with a Promise Path partner to talk about the Adventure, be sure to follow through.
• What Family Builder will you do today? Record it on page 32.

STRENGTH BUILDER
Friends want the best for their friends. And friends use the gifts God gave them to help each other, like Paul helped his friends. When you talk to your Promise Path partner (page 9), tell that person your struggles with being a Christian. Tell about things that tempt you. Ask him or her to pray for you.

TIRIPSLUA gift

His LEPH

ANSWERS: Spiritual gift; His help

WORD WALK
Read Daniel 1:1–5, 8, 11–20.

CHECK POINT

Good friends stick together during hard times. Daniel and his friends had been taken from their homes and families and taken to a strange land to live. Talk about hard times! Not only did they stick together, they also helped each other follow God's directions. Answer these questions after you have read today's Word Walk.

1. What problem did the four friends have? (Daniel 1:8)

2. How did they stick together? (1:12–13)

3. What was the result of their actions? (1:17–20)

STRENGTH BUILDER

The Path Lighter Memory Verse is about taking good advice from a friend. It is Proverbs 12:26. Read the verse on page 6, then write it in your own words.

What's the best advice a friend has given you? Write it in the speech balloon at the bottom of the page.

SKILL PRACTICE

• Use the Promise Kids Prayer in your prayer time. Thank God for the friends you have.
• Meet with a your Promise Path partner to talk about the Adventure.
• Record today's Family Builder on page 32.

THIS WAY TO
PROMISE
PATH

DAY
11

Wednesday

WORD WALK
Read James 5:13–16.

CHECK POINT
James, the writer of today's Word Walk passage, was Jesus' half brother. This passage is like a recipe for living a life that pleases God. So, let's get cracking. Use the lines to fill in the ingredients.

Add a pinch of _____(James 5:13) when you're in trouble.

Stir in a dash of _____ (5:13) when you're happy.

Add more _____ (5:14–15) when you're sick.

Don't forget to _____ (5:16) when you've sinned.

STRENGTH BUILDER
What's your recipe for a good friendship? Fill in the blanks.

SKILL PRACTICE
• Use the Promise Kid Prayer on page 2 to help you follow God's directions.
• Take another look at the Path Lighter Verse, Proverbs 12:26. What advice do you need from a friend?

• Play a song that talks about the importance of friends. For example, "Friends," by Michael W. Smith or "What a Friend We Have in Jesus." If you know the words, sing them to yourself.
• Record your Family Builder on page 32.

Add a pinch of _____ when _____.

Stir in a dash of _____ when _____.

Add more _____ when _____.

Don't forget to _____ when _____.

THIS WAY TO PROMISE PATH

Thursday

DAY 12

WORD WALK
Read 1 Samuel 20:1–7, 16–17, 19–23.

CHECK POINT
David and Jonathan were best friends. When David was in trouble, Jonathan was there to help. In fact, he risked his life to help David. That's why he's been voted "Friend of the Year" by *The Daily Blabber*. Today's Word Walk gives you the scoop. Fill in the who, what, when, where, why, and how.

The Daily Blabber

Jonathan Voted "Friend of the Year"

_____ wanted
(who? 1 Samuel 20:1)
to kill David. So David decided to skip
_____
(what? 20:5)
_____ and planned
(when? 20:5)
to hide. Jonathan wanted to help
David _____
(where? 20:5)
because _____.
(why? 20:17)
So he decided to help by _____
(how? 20:20–23)
_____.

STRENGTH BUILDER
Consider making a simple friendship bracelet for a friend as a symbol of your friendship. There are plenty of books out there with patterns. You can use yarn, string, or a leather strip. If you use beads, choose colors that mean something to you and your friend. For example, if you like the color red and your friend likes green, include those two colors on your bracelet.

SKILL PRACTICE
• During your prayer time, thank God for the people in your life whom you care about. How can you serve one of them today? (See page 11.)
• Keep trying to learn Proverbs 12:26—the Path Lighter Memory Verse.
• If you haven't met with a friend to talk about the Adventure, there's still time to do so. A brother, sister, or parent can be a Promise Path partner too!

DAY 13

This Way to Promise Path

Friday

WORD WALK
Read Ecclesiastes 4:9–12.

CHECK POINT
A breath mint advertisement on television talks about how wonderful it is to have "two, two, two mints in one." Well, today's Word Walk talks about something even more wonderful: two friends helping each other. King Solomon, one of the wisest people who ever lived, wrote Ecclesiastes. For the first question below, find three answers using the verses given.

1. Why are two people better than one? (Ecclesiastes 4:9–10, 12)

2. Now, think about a friend you have. How are you and your friend "better than one"?

STRENGTH BUILDER
Work together with a friend to help or encourage someone this week. You might do a chore for someone or make something to give away. Or, you might get a friend to help you with a pro-

ject you've been putting off. Make Ecclesiastes 4:9 your motto. Two are better than one!

SKILL PRACTICE
• Pray the Promise Kids Prayer on page 2. Prayer is one way to stop and think about Jesus.
• How has a friend helped you follow God this week?

• Keep listing those Family Builders. You'll learn more in Week 4.
• Mark where you are in the Adventure by using the chart on pages 32–33.

THIS WAY TO **PROMISE PATH**

Sat/Sun

WORD WALK
Read Hebrews 12:1–3.

CHECK POINT
No runner has ever finished a race by quitting in the middle of it. That's the message of Hebrews 12:1–3. We must PERSEVERE. That's a long word that means to never give up. The Path Lighter Verse for the week is found in this passage. You'll see parts of it popping up during the next few days. Today's part of the verse appears below. The words are a little mixed up. Number the words in the correct order.

SKILL PRACTICE
• When you pray the Promise Kids Prayer today, ask God to help you persevere through hard times.
• Clearing your path with PURITY (see page 10) will help you do what Jesus would do. Focus on a different letter of PURITY each day this week. For today, look at **P: Put away put-downs.** How can you persevere at putting aside a bad habit like putting someone down?
• Plan a time this week to be with your Promise Path partner.
• Keep listing those Family Builders.
(See page 11.)

UP IS LET GIVE RUN US AND NEVER THE

STRENGTH BUILDER
The phrase "What would Jesus do?" (WWJD) can be seen on bracelets, key rings, and cards. For this Adventure, keep in mind another phrase: "Do What Jesus Would Do" (DWJWD). If you came up with a slogan (like DWJWD) to remind you to follow Jesus, what would it be? What would the letters stand for? Write the letters on the blank bracelet.

THAT BEFORE RACE US.

Hebrews 12:1

THIS WAY TO PROMISE PATH

Monday

DAY 16

WORD WALK

Read Matthew 4:1–11.

CHECK POINT
All people are tempted to do wrong things. Being tempted is not a sin. Giving in to the temptation is. Why, even Jesus was tempted when he lived on earth. But he had a sure-fire temptation fighter that he's passed on to us. This doesn't mean we will be sinless like Jesus was, but it does mean that we can have victory over temptation.

1. What was Jesus' temptation fighter? (Matthew 4:4)

THE WINNER

2. How many times was he tempted? (Stomp your feet for the correct number.)

3. How many times did he use the temptation fighter? (Stomp your feet for the correct number.)

They make us strong for when temptation comes calling. List temptations you're facing:

SKILL PRACTICE
• During your prayer time, read your temptation list to God. Ask God to help you avoid giving in to temptation.
• Learning Scripture is one way to clear your path with PURITY. It helps you to think God's thoughts. Review the first part of the memory verse. (See page 6 for a complete listing of the Path Lighter Memory Verses.)

STRENGTH BUILDER

Facing temptation isn't easy. But there's good news! We don't have to give in. Jesus showed us the way to overcome, by using the Scriptures! That's why memorizing verses can be helpful.

WORD WALK
Read Romans 6:12, 17–18, 22–23.

CHECK POINT
Remember Paul? You read a passage of Scripture written by him (see Day 9, page 24). Today's passage is also from Romans. Below are some words you'll need in order to understand what Paul means. Match the words to the definitions.

1. Control
2. Slave
3. Sin
4. Free
5. Goodness or righteousness
6. Wages of sin

A. The wrong things we do
B. Living in obedience to God
C. Have power over
D. The results of doing wrong things
E. At liberty
F. Someone forced to serve another

Who freed us from the power of sin?

We Should _____ from _____ _____ anything that would _____ in the way. (Hebrews 12:1)

One thing that gets in my way is:

STRENGTH BUILDER
Today's section of the Path Lighter Memory Verse reminds us to put away the wrong things in our lives. In this way we are doing what Jesus would want us to do. Look at the verse on the banner at the top of the page. Some of the words have been "erased." It's up to you to supply them. Then write or draw one thing that gets in your way.

SKILL PRACTICE
• Concentrate on the R in PURITY (page 10): **Run from things you know are wrong.** What one thing do you need God's help to run from?
• Reach out in love to a family member by doing something special for him or her. Add your Family Builder to the list on pages 32–33.
• Reread the memory verse, Hebrews 12:1. You can remove wrong by telling God you're sorry. To repent means to turn from that sin. God can help you change your mind about doing wrong.

The Family Builder Adventure Log has two purposes. One is to help you keep track of where you are in the Adventure. To do this, put a check mark or an X for each day you complete in the box provided. If you have to skip a day, leave it blank. Make sure you reward yourself for reaching goals or making progress.

The second purpose of this log is to help you keep track of the Family Builders that you do each day of the Adventure. A Family Builder is one simple thing you do to serve your family. Once a week or so, your Family Builder might be to plan a fun activity your family could do together. And don't forget to include activities you try that build up your church family. For some ideas to get you started, see page 11.

❏ Day 1 _____

❏ Day 2 _____

❏ Day 3 _____

❏ Day 4 _____

❏ Day 5 _____

❏ Day 6 _____

❏ Day 7 _____

❏ Day 8 _____

❏ Day 9 _____

❏ Day 10 _____

❏ Day 11 _____

❏ Day 12 _____

❏ Day 13 _____

❏ Day 14 _____

❏ Day 15 _____

❏ Day 16 _____

❏ Day 17 _____

❏ Day 18 _____

❏ Day 19 _____

THIS WAY TO PROMISE PATH

Family Builder
Adventure Log

DAYS 20-50

❑ Day 20 _____

❑ Day 21 _____

❑ Day 22 _____

❑ Day 23 _____

❑ Day 24 _____

❑ Day 25 _____

❑ Day 26 _____

❑ Day 27 _____

❑ Day 28 _____

❑ Day 29 _____

❑ Day 30 _____

❑ Day 31 _____

❑ Day 32 _____

❑ Day 33 _____

❑ Day 34 _____

❑ Day 35 _____

❑ Day 36 _____

❑ Day 37 _____

❑ Day 38 _____

❑ Day 39 _____

❑ Day 40 _____

❑ Day 41 _____

❑ Day 42 _____

❑ Day 43 _____

❑ Day 44 _____

❑ Day 45 _____

❑ Day 46 _____

❑ Day 47 _____

❑ Day 48 _____

❑ Day 49 _____

❑ Day 50 _____

THIS WAY TO PROMISE PATH

Wednesday

DAY 18

WORD WALK
Read Psalm 119:9–16.

CHECK POINT
We're heading back through Psalm Country. For this journey, the Word Walk gives advice on what you can do to follow God's directions. However, when writing the directions, someone got confused. Rewrite these tips for following God. Then make up an action for each tip. This will help you to remember them.

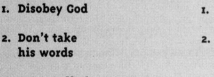

1. Disobey God	1.
2. Don't take his words	2.
3. Never tell about the laws God has spoken	3.
4. Never think about God's orders	4.
5. Grumble and complain when obeying God's orders	5.
6. Forget God's Word	6.

mix up the order of the cards. Try to put them in the correct order. Invite a family member to join you. This is a good way to make sure you don't forget God's Word.

SKILL PRACTICE
• The Word Walk passage has lots of suggestions for how to clear your path with PURITY. For today, concentrate on **U: Undo unkind actions.** This means saying you're sorry when you do something unkind. Also work on **I: Invite an adult who loves you to help you.**
• Record your Family Builder on page 32.

STRENGTH BUILDER
Review those portions of the memory verse that were covered earlier in the week. To practice the verse, write each word on an index card. Then

DAY
19

THIS WAY TO PROMISE PATH

Thursday

WORD WALK
Read Colossians 3:8–10, 12–15.

CHECK POINT
Today Paul has some clothing advice. But he's not talking about clothes made of fabric. He's talking about attitudes we can put on or take off each day. We need to take off bad attitudes and wrong actions and put on attitudes and actions that please God. On the T-shirts, write or draw the things Paul says we need to take off and the things we need to put on.

STRENGTH BUILDER
"Taking off" the bad things in our lives is what the Path Lighter Memory Verse (Hebrews 12:1–2) is about. But the vowels are covered with spots. You'll need a good "spot" remover to read the verse. Write in the correct vowels.

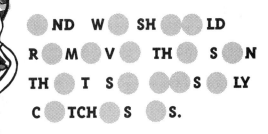

◯ND W◯SH◯◯LD
R◯M◯V◯ TH◯ S◯N
TH◯T S◯ ◯◯S◯LY
C◯TCH◯S ◯S.

Take Off

Put On

SKILL PRACTICE
• As you clear your path with PURITY, **Think God's thoughts** (the T in PURITY). This reminds you to think *What would Jesus do?* in the situations you find most tempting. Then try to do what he would do.
• Use the Promise Kids Prayer during your prayer time. Do you need God's help to take off a bad attitude?
• Did you do a Family Builder today? Write it on page 32.

THIS WAY TO PROMISE PATH

Friday

DAY 20

WORD WALK
Read Philippians 4:8–9.

CHECK POINT
We end the week with more of Paul's advice. This time, he's talking about what we put in our minds by what we watch, hear, read, and think. What have you put into your mind today? Write or draw some of those things in the thought balloon. Circle the ones that match the descriptions of good things Paul says we need to be thinking about. Use an X to mark out the things that are not good to put into your mind.

STRENGTH BUILDER
The advice of today's portion of the Path Lighter Verse (Hebrews 12:1–2) can help you think good thoughts. Hold this page up to the mirror to find out what the advice is.

"Let us look only to Jesus".
Hebrews 12:2

SKILL PRACTICE
• As you clear your path with PURITY, don't forget to **Yell for joy.** Celebrate whenever you triumph over temptation, even in small ways.
• See if you can say the whole Path Lighter Verse for this week: Hebrews 12:1–2.

• List your Family Builder on page 33.
• Have you talked to your Promise Path partner this week? Why not tell him or her what you've learned about PURITY?

DAYS 21/22

THIS WAY TO PROMISE PATH

Sat/Sun

WORD WALK
Read Matthew 20:20–28.

CHECK POINT
Moms want what's best for their kids. And James and John's mother certainly wanted that for her boys. James and John were already two of Jesus' closest friends. She wanted them to be important men. Sitting on the right and left hand of a king meant that a person had power and importance. But Jesus wanted people to consider another path toward greatness. Interview one or two people. Ask them these questions:

1. What is the world's definition of greatness?

2. What is Jesus' definition of greatness?

STRENGTH BUILDER
This week we'll be talking a lot about families. Have you been doing Family Builders each day? If not, read page 11 about things you can do to serve your family members.

What will you do today and for whom?

SKILL PRACTICE
• Pray the Promise Kids Prayer. As you do, remember to thank God for the family he has given you.
• Work on building up your family with Family Builders. Use the chart on pages 32–33 to record your acts of service.
• Begin work on learning Ephesians 6:2–3—this week's Path Lighter Memory Verse. Try putting the words to a familiar tune and sing the verse.

THIS WAY TO **PROMISE PATH**

Monday

DAY 23

WORD WALK
Read Esther 2:5–11.

CHECK POINT
Families come in all different sizes and kinds. Some people don't live with a mom or dad. But they're just as loved as if they did. Esther didn't have parents who were living. But she did have a loving relative who helped her. And eventually Esther became a queen.

What is your family like? Draw a picture of them in the empty frame.

STRENGTH BUILDER
This week's Path Lighter Verse is Ephesians 6:2–3. But some words of the first part of this passage have faded out. Can you figure out the missing words?

_____ **your father** _____ **mother. This is** _____ **first commandment that has a** _____ **with it.**

(Note: Even though the verse reads "father" and "mother," you may not live with either one. If this is true for you, then make sure you do what the verse says to do for the person who is taking care of you.)

Now, take another look at the first word of the memory verse. What does it mean to you?

SKILL PRACTICE
• Take the Path Lighter Verse to heart by doing something to honor a parent or guardian today. You might think of doing a chore without having to be told to do it. Or, make him or her a card to express your love. That's your Family Builder for today.
• Plan a time this week to talk with your Promise Path partner. (See page 9.)

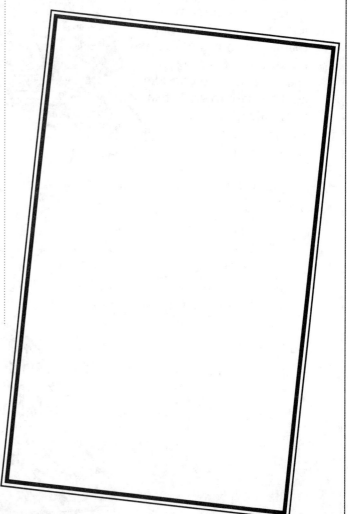

THIS WAY TO PROMISE PATH

Tuesday

DAY 24

WORD WALK
Read Ephesians 6:1–4.

CHECK POINT
This week we're talking about important family stuff. In today's Word Walk, the apostle Paul tells how family members can get along with each other. *Reading* what Paul wrote is one thing. *Doing* something about it is better.

1. According to Ephesians 6:1–2. What are two commandments you need to do?

2. What action can you take to show that you are obeying these commandments?

3. In verse 4, where Paul is writing to fathers (and moms, grandparents, etc.), what do you think Paul means? Circle the best answer.

A. Parents should never do anything that will result in a child's being angry.

B. Parents should not do anything intentionally to make their children angry or expect their children to do things that are beyond their ability.

Parents and other adults need to do things that are best for their children, even if their children choose to be angry. Remember that the next time your mom or dad says no to you.

Generally, children should honor their parents by obeying them. But if a parent asks a child to do something that is wrong, then God does not expect the child to obey.

STRENGTH BUILDER
The Path Lighter Memory Verse is part of today's Word Walk passage. The first part was given yesterday. The second part is given today. But we still have some faded words!

> _____ _____ is: "Then _____
>
> will be well _____ you."
>
> (Ephesians 6:3)

SKILL PRACTICE

• What Family Builder will you try today to honor a parent as Ephesians 6:2–3 commands? Don't forget to list it on page 33.
• When you pray the Promise Kids Prayer today, ask God to help you be willing to follow his directions, even when it's hard.

THIS WAY TO PROMISE PATH

Wednesday

DAY 25

WORD WALK
Read Genesis 50:15–21.

CHECK POINT
The family in today's Word Walk passage had had a feud. Ten of Joseph's brothers had sold Joseph as a slave. Joseph had been taken to Egypt. While a slave, Joseph was thrown wrongfully into prison. One day, the pharaoh had a dream he couldn't understand. After Joseph told the pharaoh what the dream meant, Joseph became one of the most important men in Egypt. (See chapters 37, 39—41 for the whole story.) Well, Joseph forgave his brothers for what they did. But when their father Jacob died, the brothers became afraid.

STRENGTH BUILDER
Suppose you could rent space on a billboard to tell everyone about your family. What would you put on it? Use the blank billboard provided.

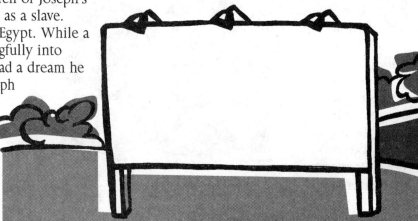

1. What did the brothers think that Joseph would do to them? (Genesis 50:15)

2. How did Joseph comfort them? (50:19—21)

SKILL PRACTICE
• Build up good feelings within your family by working on Family Builders. Use the list on pages 32—33 to keep track.
• If you've hurt someone in your family, make things right. When you pray the Promise Kids Prayer, ask God to help you forgive like Joseph did.

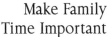

THIS WAY TO **PROMISE PATH**

Thursday

DAY 26

WORD WALK
Read Deuteronomy 6:4–9.

CHECK POINT
God told Moses to tell the people of Israel, "Listen up!" God wanted them to listen to his commands. And he wanted them to remember and obey them.
How were parents to teach their children about the commands? (Deuteronomy 6:6–9) Draw a line through the items in the list that aren't in the passage. Add to the list a way for you to remember God's commands.

1. Talk about them when you're at home or walking along the road.
2. Ignore the ones you don't like.
3. Talk about them when you lie down and get up.
4. Write them down.
5. Tie them to your hands.
6. Tie them to your forehead.
7. Tie them around your waist.
8. Write them on your doors and gates.

9. _____.

STRENGTH BUILDER
Memorizing the Path Lighter Memory Verses is a good start to remembering God's directions. Reread Ephesians 6:2–3. Then answer the following:

1. What do you do when you need to remember something important?

2. What will you do to remember the meaning of this week's memory verse?

3. Name a Bible verse you learned that helped you in a time of need.

SKILL PRACTICE
• Are you remembering to build up your family through kind acts? Don't forget to help plan a fun activity your family can all do together. That's a way to make family time important.
• Pray the Promise Kids Prayer. Ask God to help you be obedient to him.
• Mark where you are in the Adventure by using the chart on pages 32–33.

THIS WAY TO
PROMISE PATH

DAY
27

Friday

WORD WALK
Read 2 Samuel 9:1–10.

CHECK POINT
After reading today's Word Walk, use the clues below to solve the crossword puzzle. As you do, think about how David's concern for others included not only his family members, but those around him too.

STRENGTH BUILDER
God gives each of us a family to love. God also wants us to treat our friends and their families with kindness, just like (1 Across) did for (3 Across). What kind thing can you do today for a friend's family?

SKILL PRACTICE
• As you read the Promise Kids Prayer, consider praying for each of your family members.
• Keep working on those Family Builders. You might consider choosing a fun activity for your family to do together.
• Try to say (or sing) the Path Lighter Verse, Ephesians 6:2–3, from memory.
• Have you talked to your Promise Path partner yet this week? What did you talk about?

(1 Across) wanted to do something nice for (3 Across), the son of his friend (2 Down). (You read about [1 Across] and [2 Down] on Day 12.) (3 Across) was crippled in both (4 Down). (1 Across) decided to give (3 Across) back his family's land. (1 Across) treated (3 Across) like he was a member of (1 Across)'s own family. That's why (1 Across) decided to always save a place for (3 Across) at his (5 Down).

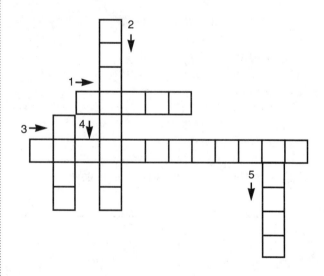

ANSWERS: Across: (1) David; (3) Mephibosheth. Down: (2) Jonathan; (4) feet; (5) table.

THIS WAY TO PROMISE PATH

Sat/Sun

DAYS
28/29

WORD WALK
Read Ephesians 4:11–13, 16.

CHECK POINT
You know about the five food groups, right? Eating foods from these groups can help build strong bodies. There are five other things that build a strong body, too. But not your physical body. I'm talking about the body of Christ—the church. All Christians together make up the body of Christ. Today's Word Walk passage tells about five of the gifts God gave to help Christians build up the body of Christ. These are called *spiritual gifts*. They help other Christians learn how to follow God's directions. Write the five gifts. Then match each gift with its definition by writing its letter after the appropriate word.

What are the five gifts?

1.

2.

3.

4.

5.

Definitions
A. One who shares the good news of Jesus with others

B. One who is sent on a mission (The disciples were also called this.)

C. One who tells the people God's words (also called a seer)

D. A church leader who cares for a church congregation and helps them follow God's directions

E. One who teaches or trains others

STRENGTH BUILDER
Even if you don't have one of the gifts listed in Ephesians 4, you can still help make the body of Christ strong. Check off below something you plan to do this week. Or, write your own suggestion on the line provided.

❏ I'll pray for someone in my church family.

❏ I'll write an encouraging note to my pastor.

❏ I'll help my teacher this week.

❏ I'll_____.

SKILL PRACTICE
• Begin working on learning the Path Lighter Memory Verse, Hebrews 10:25. Try doing the verse like a cheer.

• Think about ways you can "build up" your church family. See page 11 for God's Family Builder suggestions. Once you've thought about what to do, the next step is to do it!

• Keep listing your Family Builders on pages 32–33. During this week, do some Family Builders for your church.

ANSWERS: Apostles (B); prophets (C); evangelists (A); pastors (D); teachers (E)

Get Involved
at Church

THIS WAY TO PROMISE PATH

Monday

WORD WALK
Read 1 Thessalonians 5:12–13.

CHECK POINT
A person in the army salutes to show his or her respect for leaders. Well, we're to respect our leaders too. But we don't have to salute! God just wants us to appreciate the hard work they put into building up the body of Christ. To review what you have read, do the following:

Look up the word *respect* in the dictionary. Write the definition.	Write the definition in your own words.
_____	_____
_____	_____
_____	_____

Now, think of one of your church leaders. This might be your pastor, youth director, church secretary, or Sunday school teacher. List some of the tasks that person does each week.

STRENGTH BUILDER
A leader's job isn't easy. Consider making a card or another gift to tell your

pastor, teacher, or other leader what you respect and appreciate about him or her. Or, when you see this person in church, give him or her a hug!

SKILL PRACTICE
• This week, make a special effort to get involved at church. Is there a ministry your church sponsors where you can get involved? For example, a food pantry, homeless ministry, drama group, and so on? How will you get involved in what's going on at your church?
• Work on learning the Path Lighter Memory Verse, Hebrews 10:25.
• Don't forget to list your church Family Builders on pages 32–33.
• Plan a time to talk with your Promise Path partner.

44

DAY 31

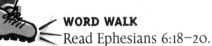

WORD WALK
Read Ephesians 6:18–20.

CHECK POINT
What's one of the things all Christians need? **РRAYERS FOR OTHERS** (Hold this paper up to the mirror to find out!) We can talk to God ourselves. But God also tells us to pray for each other. How often should we pray? Color the spaces where the sum is an even number to find out.

STRENGTH BUILDER
Keep a list of people to pray for within your church family. Be sure to include your church leaders. In one column you can write what the person needs. In another column, you can write what answer your prayer received.

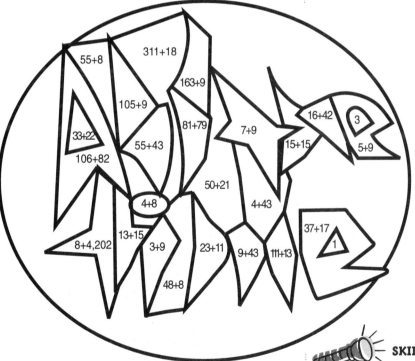

55+8
311+18
163+9
105+9
81+79
16+42
3
7+9
15+15
5+9
33+22
55+43
106+82
50+21
4+8
4+43
13+15
37+17
8+4,202
3+9
23+11
9+43
111+13
1
48+8

SKILL PRACTICE
• Keep working on learning the Path Lighter Memory Verse, Hebrews 10:25.
• How are you coming with your church Family Builders? Write what you did on page 33.
• Are you getting more involved at church?

ANSWER: All the time

THIS WAY TO **PROMISE PATH**

Wednesday

DAY 32

WORD WALK
Read Hebrews 10:24–25.

CHECK POINT
When was the last time anyone said to you, "You can do it" when you were facing a hard task? You probably felt like you could complete the task, didn't you? That's the message of today's Word Walk. We can help each other do good things. That's what being part of the family of God is all about. We can do good things—together! Write your answers to the following questions:

1. What are some things you like to do with the people in your church?

2. Take a look at this week's Path Lighter Memory Verse. The verse is part of today's Word Walk. (The verse is printed on page 6.) Make a poster telling why it is important to meet together as Christians. Perhaps you could hang your poster in a hallway at church.

STRENGTH BUILDER
Our words and actions can send a clear message of love to others. Speaking of messages, check out the code below. Use it to find out what we can do to help others.

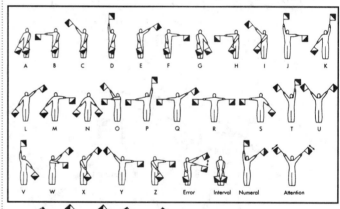

__ __ __ __ __ __ __ __ __ **others.**

Who will you do this for this week?

SKILL PRACTICE
• Don't forget to list your Family Builders and God's Family Builders on pages 32–33. Think about calling your Sunday school teacher to thank him or her for teaching your class.
• Think of church as a place where you can go to grow. What are some ways your church has helped you grow as a Christian?
• Don't forget to use the Promise Kids Prayer.
• Have you marked where you are in the Adventure on pages 32–33?

ANSWER: Encourage

THIS WAY TO PROMISE PATH

Thursday

DAY 33

WORD WALK

Read Exodus 35:20–22, 29; 36:2–4.

CHECK POINT
While the people of Israel wandered in the wilderness on their way to the promised land, they needed a place to worship God. God told Moses how to build the Tabernacle, a place of worship. The people gave what they had to build the Tabernacle. Gold earrings and bracelets, fabric, and sheep and goat skins were given.

STRENGTH BUILDER
There are some gifts we can give to help others worship God too.
Unscramble the words to see what the gifts are. Add one of your own if you'd like. Then circle the gift you will work at giving.

emti _____   stnaelt _____

meyon _____   eplh_____

Other _____

1. Why do you think the people wanted to give?

2. Do the gifts people in your church give help your church? How?

SKILL PRACTICE
• Have you learned the Path Lighter Memory Verse, Hebrews 10:25?
* Don't forget to include a church Family Builder in your plans this week.
• Pray about what you can do to get more involved at church.

ANSWERS: time; talents; money; help.

THIS WAY TO **PROMISE PATH**

Friday

DAY 34

WORD WALK
Read 2 Corinthians 8:1–4, 7–9.

CHECK POINT
Today's Word Walk comes from a letter written to the church in the ancient city of Corinth. (Corinth is in the country of Greece.) The apostle Paul wanted to remind these first-century Christians (and us) to be generous. We can all be generous in some way. Draw a line to match the questions to the answers.

1. Who gave to Paul? (2 Corinthians 8:1–3)

Jesus, salvation.

2. We give because someone first gave to us. Who? What was given? (8:9)

Because God instructs us to do this.

3. Why is it good to give to others?

Macedonian churches

STRENGTH BUILDER
God wants you to be generous. But there is one gift he wants you to give before you give anything else. Write every other letter, starting with the first one, to find out what that is.

YEORPULR SSFETL F G

SKILL PRACTICE
• End the week with a prayer of thanks for your church family. Then pray about ways you can give to help out the ministries of your church.
• Impress your family with your learning of Hebrews 10:25, the Path Lighter Memory Verse. If you made up a cheer, teach it to them. Then talk about ways to do what the verse says.
• Don't forget to build up your church family this week with a God's Family Builder.
• Have you talked to your Promise Path partner this week? Tell him or her what you are learning on the Adventure.

ANSWER: Yourself

48

WORD WALK
Read Luke 10:25–37.

CHECK POINT
In Jesus' day, the Israelites and the Samaritans didn't get along. The Israelites even avoided traveling in towns where Samaritans lived! Imagine everyone's surprise when Jesus told a story featuring a Samaritan who helped a Jewish man! This story is known as the "Parable of the Good Samaritan."

Suppose you were making a movie of this story. If you had to come up with another title, what would you name it? Write your idea on the blank screen.

Suppose this story took place today in your neighborhood. Instead of Israelites and Samaritans, what kinds of people would be involved? Why? Would the end of the story be different? Talk these questions over with a parent or friend.

STRENGTH BUILDER
People today have trouble getting along, just like the Israelites and the Samaritans did. Many times problems result because we don't know each other well. It's easy to fear someone you don't know. Pray about fears you have concerning people of other races or cultures. Ask God to help you reach put and be a "good Samaritan" to someone from another culture.

SKILL PRACTICE
• This week's Path Lighter Verse helps us to know the way God sees all people. The verse, 1 Samuel 16:7, is printed on page 6. How can you make this verse your motto this week?
• Make plans to learn about another race or culture. You might go to the library and check out books, learn from the Internet, or watch a video. See page 12 for more information.
• And don't forget to record your Family Builder on page 33.

Accept Others
as Jesus Does

WORD WALK
Read Mark 1:40–42.

CHECK POINT
In Jesus' day, people were terrified of leprosy. It was a contagious, dangerous disease. As a result, lepers were often made to leave their family and friends and to live alone or with other lepers. But Jesus wasn't afraid of the lepers. He knew that these people who were "different" needed love and friendship, too. Pretend you are an on-the-spot reporter as you write or draw answers to these questions.

1. How did the man feel when Jesus reached out to him? How did the man show his feelings?

2. What did the people watching do when they saw Jesus touch the man?

3. How did Jesus feel toward the man with leprosy? How did Jesus show his feelings?

STRENGTH BUILDER
As we learn to know and accept people who are different from us, we are not comparing these people to the lepers in the Bible story. The lepers merely represented people no one wanted for friends. There are kids in your school and church whom no one may want for friends either. This is because we often judge a person by how he or she looks. But, this week's Path Lighter Memory Verse tells us how God sees people. The verse, 1 Samuel 16:7, is on page 6. What do you think God sees in your heart concerning your feelings about people who are different from you? Fill in the heart with words or a picture that describes what's in your heart. What, if anything, needs to change?

SKILL PRACTICE
• Follow through on any plans you've made to learn about a race or culture different from your own. For ideas, see page 12.
• Ask God to help you show Jesus' acceptance to others. If you have trouble seeing past someone's looks or personality, ask God to help you see what's special about that person.

THIS WAY TO PROMISE PATH

Tuesday

DAY 38

WORD WALK
Read John 4:5–14, 25–29, 39, 42.

CHECK POINT
Earlier in the week you learned about the Samaritans. In today's Word Walk Jesus did more than tell a story about Samaritans. He talked to one! No big deal, right? Wrong. Remember, the Jews went out of their way to avoid the Samaritans. Also, in Jesus' day, men didn't talk to women in public.

STRENGTH BUILDER
Jesus took time to talk to the Samaritan woman. In fact, he started the conversation. Is there someone you'd feel embarrassed to be seen talking to in a public place? Think about a kid in your school or neighborhood whom other kids ignore. What can you do to show that person you accept him or her as Jesus does? When will you do this?

SKILL PRACTICE
• Accepting others as Jesus does includes reaching out to people others may not accept. Try it!

• Don't forget the message of this week's Path Lighter Memory Verse, 1 Samuel 16:7. God sees beyond what a person looks like. How can you see others that way? Speaking of the memory verse, how are you coming along in learning it?

• Add another Family Builder to the list on pages 32–33. Show family members that you accept them as Jesus does.

• Don't forget to use the Promise Kids Prayer. Ask God to help you follow his directions as you learn to appreciate those who are different from you.

So there Jesus was, talking to a Samaritan woman in a public place! What do you think the disciples thought when they saw this scene? Write the thoughts in the spaces provided. Then draw what you think their faces may have looked like.

What do you think Jesus wanted his disciples and us to learn from this?

Accept Others
as Jesus Does

THIS WAY TO PROMISE PATH

Wednesday

WORD WALK
Read Mark 9:33–41.

CHECK POINT
A famous boxer once claimed that he was "the Greatest." His claim to fame was that he was faster, stronger, and meaner than other boxers. Other people have wondered who the greatest is, too. Jesus' disciples even wanted to know who was the greatest among their group! (You read about a similar discussion on Days 21/22.) Jesus had a surprising answer about how to be the greatest. Unscramble the three words to figure out his answer.

E B / A / E N A R S T V

If you do what Jesus says, how will that change the way you treat others? List two specific changes you could make.

1.

2.

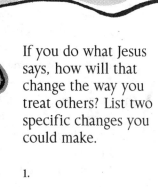

STRENGTH BUILDER
We can reach out to all kinds of people as Jesus would do. You might volunteer to read a story to a little kid or spend some time with an elderly person. Go out of your way to look for people you might normally overlook.

SKILL PRACTICE
• When you pray today, ask God to show you ways you can be kind to others. Be open to showing kindness to all types of people.
• If you've learned this week's Path Lighter Verse, 1 Samuel 16:7, say it to yourself using a clap rhythm.
• Don't forget to record your Family Builders (see page 11 and Week 4).
• When will you talk to your Promise Path partner this week (see page 9)?

ANSWER: Be a servant

52

THIS WAY TO PROMISE PATH

Thursday

DAY 40

WORD WALK
Read Matthew 25:31–39, 40–41, 45.

CHECK POINT
Jesus was telling his listeners about what would happen at a future time. God will judge the things we do for others. Jesus used animals his listeners knew about to help them understand his message. Sheep represent the followers of Jesus. The goats represent those who say they follow Jesus, but their actions don't show that they do. Review the Word Walk by answering these questions.

1. What did the sheep do that the goats didn't do? (Matthew 25:37–39, 45)

2. Who are some people today who are like the people in this passage? Think about those who are sick or who don't have enough food or clothes. Is it ever hard for you to accept them? If so, why?

3. Circle your honest response. How would your actions change knowing that helping others is the same as helping Jesus?

I'd do more to help.
I'd do less to help.
My actions would stay the same.

STRENGTH BUILDER
Reaching out and accepting others is just one part of being a sheep—a follower of Jesus. It's also not something you can do once and then you're done. You need to practice this daily. To remind yourself to follow Jesus, sign the SHEEP card. At the end of the Adventure, cut out the card and place it where you will see it. By signing, you're saying you want to do what sheep do—follow Jesus. What will be your first action as an official member of SHEEP?

Sheep
_____
Your Name

Helping

Everyone

Everywhere

Positively

SKILL PRACTICE
• What plans have you made to learn about another race or culture? Don't forget to do something about those plans. If you need ideas, see page 12.
• Did you do a Family Builder today? Record it on pages 32–33.

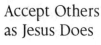

WORD WALK
Read Psalm 19:12–14.

CHECK POINT
Grab a mirror or stand in front of one. If you're facing the mirror, can you see the back of your head? No. The back of your head is like the "hidden side" of the moon—you can't see it. There is also a "hidden or secret part" of our lives, according to this psalm. On the paper, draw the images that come to your mind as you reread these verses.

STRENGTH BUILDER
Sometimes the secret attitudes of our hearts keep us from accepting others. Take a moment to ask God to show you any hidden thoughts that keep you from accepting others as Jesus does. God's Word helps bring the hidden side into the light. Read the Path Lighter Verse or say it to yourself, if you learned it. God is an expert at knowing the good and bad things inside each person's heart. If there are bad things, he will forgive you and help you to get rid of them. All you need to do is ask.

SKILL PRACTICE
• Take a look at the Promise Kids Prayer on page 2. If you're having trouble accepting others as Jesus does, admit it in prayer today. Remember, God sees the heart.
• Keep learning 1 Samuel 16:7, the Path Lighter Verse. If you've already learned it, great! What have you learned about another race or culture this week?

WORD WALK

Read Matthew 28:19–20; Mark 12:30–31.

CHECK POINT

Officers in the army or navy tell their troops what to do. These commands are known as marching orders. Officers expect their people to obey, not just listen. Jesus expects the same thing from us—to do what he says. The commands in the Word Walk passages are our marching orders.

These commands are known as the Great Commission (Matthew 28:19–20) and the Great Commandment (Mark 12:30–31). Both are tied to one thing—love. The Great Commandment repeats a command you read about on Day 26. Check out the following definition. Then write or draw answers to the questions.

Disciple: One who follows Jesus

Our marching orders: (Matthew 28:19–20)
What is one way you can do this through the missions programs in your church?

Our marching orders: (Mark 12:30–31)
What is one way you can do this?

STRENGTH BUILDER

On a piece of paper draw a map of your "world." Include the location of your home, school, and the boundaries of your neighborhood. How can the good news of Jesus make a difference where you are?

SKILL PRACTICE

• Making a difference means being aware of the needs in your neighborhood, then doing something to help. Think about things you and your friends can do to make a difference in your neighborhood.

• Look back at the Promise Kids Prayer on page 2. What is one way you want God to help you make a difference at home? (Perhaps you could do something as a regular Family Builder.) With people of other cultures?

• Check out the Path Lighter Verse, Matthew 5:16, on page 6.

THIS WAY TO PROMISE PATH

Monday

DAY 44

WORD WALK
Read Acts 8:26–35.

CHECK POINT
What's a big change that's happened in your life? For an Ethiopian ruler, his meeting with one of Jesus' disciples led to a big change in his life. But the change probably didn't stop there. The ruler probably went home and told his friends and family what had happened to him. So, the change in the Ehtiopian's life probably affected the lives of many others, too. To review the story, use your Bible to answer these questions:

1. How did Philip know where to go?

2. How did the Ethiopian ruler show his belief?

STRENGTH BUILDER
Knowing Jesus made a difference in the Ethiopian ruler's life. How does knowing Jesus make a difference in your life? On the T-shirt at the top of the page, write or draw a message you'd like to share with someone in another country or from another culture.

SKILL PRACTICE
• Jesus can make a difference in anyone's life, just as he did in the Ethiopian ruler's life. If you're still not certain how God makes a difference, talk to a parent or a pastor. Don't be embarrassed to ask questions.
• Friends make a difference in each other's lives by spending time together. In order for God to make a difference in your life, you need to spend time with him. As you stop and think about Jesus, you learn more about what he wants for your life. That can help you make a difference in someone else's life.
• Be sure to record your Family Builders on page 33.

THIS WAY TO PROMISE PATH

Tuesday

WORD WALK
Read Matthew 5:13–16.

CHECK POINT
Jesus spoke these words during his Sermon on the Mount. He wanted his listeners to know how to make a difference in the world. So he told them about salt and light. Salt wakes up the flavor of everything it's added to. A little bit can make a big difference. And light—well, you know the difference light makes if you have ever been lost in the dark woods. Being salt and light means that we are to do what Jesus would do and share our beliefs about him. As salt and light, we can share the message that Jesus died for our sins.

What concerns you about being "salt and light"? Put a check next to the one that describes a worry you have. (Be honest!) Then talk it over with a parent or a friend. Don't forget to pray about it!

___ **My friends thinking I'm weird**
___ **Having to talk about God and not knowing what to say**
___ **Not really knowing what difference Jesus makes in someone's life**
___ **Other** _____
_____
_____

STRENGTH BUILDER
This week's Path Lighter Verse, Matthew 5:16, is part of the Word Walk passage. Read that verse in your Bible or on page 6. Then finish each sentence below to tell how God helps you be "light" in a dark world.

Being light means . . .

The good things I do that others can see are . . .

I want people to praise my Father in heaven for . . .

SKILL PRACTICE
• Ask God to help you face any fears you might have about telling others about Jesus.
• Pray for someone who needs to hear about Jesus.
• Thank God for the people who were "salt" and "light" in your life. Don't forget to thank them!
• Did you remember to do a Family Builder?
• Try to talk to your Promise Path partner about your concerns in regard to today's lesson.

THIS WAY TO PROMISE PATH

Wednesday

DAY 46

WORD WALK
Read Matthew 9:35–38.

CHECK POINT
When companies need workers, they usually advertise in newspapers, on radios, or the Internet. None of these things existed in Jesus' day. But Jesus wanted everyone to know that a job was available. What was the job? Who has the "right stuff" for the job? Fill in the ad.

STRENGTH BUILDER
A person who wants a job usually has a resume. The resume helps an employer know what the person can do. If you want to apply for the job described in Matthew 9:35–38, you need to tell what you can do. Fill in the resume.

Wanted: (Matthew 9:37)

Main quality Jesus is looking for:

Resume for _____

My Gifts and Talents:
(Place a check beside the gifts or talents you have. If your talent isn't listed, write it on the line provided.)

❏ Encourage others
❏ Sing or play an instrument
❏ Draw
❏ Write
❏ Dance
❏ Play a sport
Other:

How I could use these talents to make a difference in someone's life: (For example: You could write a story. Then you could tell it to the younger children in your neighborhood.)

SKILL PRACTICE
• During your prayer time, ask God to help you use your gifts and talents to make a difference in someone's life.
• Reread the Path Lighter Verse, Matthew 5:16. How have you shown by your actions that you are "light"?
• Remember to do a Family Builder and record it on page 33.

ANSWERS: Workers for the harvest; compassion

THIS WAY TO **PROMISE PATH**

Thursday

DAY 47

WORD WALK
Read 2 Corinthians 5:14–15, 17, 19–20.

CHECK POINT
An ambassador represents his or her home country. Wherever an ambassador goes, he or she acts in the name of that country. As Jesus' ambassadors, we act in his name. That means we have his authority or power to back us up. And we represent our real homeland, heaven. God wants us to take his message of peace to people all over world.

How could you spread Jesus' message of peace this week?

Someone once described what it's like to know or not know Jesus: "No Jesus, no peace. Know Jesus, know peace." Make up your own slogan to describe what it's like to know Jesus.

STRENGTH BUILDER
As Jesus' ambassador, you don't have to travel to make a difference in the lives of people all over the world. If you were giving a speech to a group of kids to encourage them to get involved in missions, what would you say? Write your speech notes in the space provided. You might try out this speech with a friend or family member.

Speech Notes

SKILL PRACTICE
• It takes time to make a difference in someone's life. Some changes don't happen overnight. Think about the things God has done in your life over the past 50 days. You can tell others what God has done.
• Knowing that you can make a difference in someone's life is the first step toward doing something about it. What will you do?
• Keep learning the Path Lighter Verse, Matthew 5:16.
• Record a Family Builder on page 33.

THIS WAY TO PROMISE PATH

DAY 48

Friday

WORD WALK
Read 2 Corinthians 4:8–9,
13–15, 18.

CHECK POINT
For the last few days, we've talked about making a difference. There is one event that makes a big difference to all of our lives: Jesus died for our sins and then rose from the grave. Knowing that Jesus lives can give us hope for the future. The apostle Paul knew this. That's why he was able to stand up to the trouble of the present. What are your present troubles? What do you worry about concerning the future? Write a letter to Paul expressing your concerns. Then go back to the Word Walk passage. Write the good advice Paul gives.

"the future"

Dear Paul:

Signed,
Worried and Troubled

Dear Worried and Troubled:

Signed,
Paul

STRENGTH BUILDER
Keeping on the Promise Path means knowing how to live one day at a time. That means giving God our worries concerning the future. If you wrote your letter of worries about the future, take time to bring those worries to God.

SKILL PRACTICE
• This week's Path Lighter Memory Verse is Psalm 16:11. You can find the verse listed on page 6.
• Don't forget your Family Builders (see Week 4 and page 11). Keep listing them on page 33. How many do you have?

Saturday

WORD WALK
Read Philippians 3:10–14.

CHECK POINT
Have you ever watched the Olympics? It is amazing how the athletes who participate work and train so hard for this one event. There is suffering involved as well. And why do they do this? For the prize of an Olympic gold medal. The apostle Paul felt the same way about the prize he wanted. He was willing to suffer to gain it. And he suffered a lot! What was the prize? Eternal life with Jesus and the rewards that wait for us.

1. What did Paul want to know? (Philipians 3:10)

2. One way to know Jesus is to stop and think about him every day. How will you do that after this Adventure?

STRENGTH BUILDER

Speaking of knowing, here's something you should know: the Path Lighter Verse, Psalm 16:11. Solve the rebus.

SKILL PRACTICE
• Pray the Promise Kids Prayer. As you do, think about your goals for the future. Ask God to help you follow his directions one day at a time.
• Say the Path Lighter Memory Verse, Psalm 16:11, to yourself or someone else several times.
• Don't forget your Family Builders. Why not plan something fun you could do with your family to celebrate finishing the Adventure?

ANSWER: You will teach me God's way to live. Being with you will fill me with joy. At your right hand I will find pleasure forever.

THIS WAY TO PROMISE PATH

Sunday

DAY 50

WORD WALK
Read Luke 24:1–12.

CHECK POINT
The people who followed Jesus probably thought all hope had died. After all, Jesus was dead. They had seen him buried. But early on Sunday morning, something amazing happened. Draw what their faces might have looked like that morning.

What do you believe, based on their report? Write your answer in the thought balloon or tell it to a friend or parent.

I believe that:

STRENGTH BUILDER
What if . . . Jesus had not come back to life? Maybe you've asked yourself that question. But the truth is, he did! Knowing the truth about Jesus' resurrection helps keep us on the Promise Path. Because Jesus lives, all those who love him will live forever with him someday. His presence, through the Holy Spirit, helps us live each day with hope and power. Don't forget that Jesus walks along the path with you. He'll never leave you alone!

SKILL PRACTICE
• You did it! You made it through the Adventure. That's worth celebrating. And remember, the Adventure isn't over. This is just part of the journey. Keeping on the Promise Path means trying to follow God's directions each day.
• Did you learn Psalm 16:11, the Path Lighter Memory Verse? If not, make that your goal for today. You can find the verse listed on page 6.
• Although you may record your last Family Builder on line 50, don't make that your last one ever. Keep on building up your family and church members.
• Get together with your Promise Path partner to talk about what you've learned on the Adventure. How could you and your partner keep helping each other follow Jesus?

Promise Kids Resources

Item	Title	Price	Quantity	Total
VeggieTales® Videos				
8441	Larry-Boy! and the Fib from Outer Space!	$15.00	_____	_____
8431	Rack, Shack & Benny	$15.00	_____	_____
8425	Are You My Neighbor?	$15.00	_____	_____
8419	"God Wants Me to Forgive Them?!?"	$15.00	_____	_____
8312	"Where's God When I'm Scared?"	$15.00	_____	_____
50-Day Spiritual Adventure Journals				
2930	Son Power for Super Kids	$6.00	_____	_____
2730	G. H. Construction Crew	$6.00	_____	_____
2630	Adventure Gear for God's Kids	$6.00	_____	_____

	Subtotal	$_____
Add 10% for UPS shipping/handling ($4.00 minimum)		$_____
Canadian or Illinois residents add 7% GST/sales tax		$_____
Total (subtotal + shipping + tax)		$_____
	Total Amount Enclosed	$_____

Ship my order to:

Child's Name _____ Age _____

Parent's Name _____

Street Address* _____

City _____ State/Prov _____ Zip/Code _____

*Note: UPS will not deliver to a P.O. box.

Mail this order form with your check to:
Mainstay Church Resources, Box 30, Wheaton, IL 60189-0030
In Canada: The Chapel Ministries, Box 2000, Waterdown, ON L0R 2H0
For VISA, MasterCard, or Discover Card orders call 1-800-224-2735 (U.S.) or 1-800-461-4114 (Canada).

M089CG

4 VeggieTales Videos

You may not like to eat vegetables, but you'll love the vegetable characters in these videos. Lots of other kids like them, too, because **VeggieTales®** is the number one selling Christian video series. Pick from four great episodes:

- *Rack, Shack, and Benny*—The story of Shadrach, Meshach, and Abednego like you've never seen it before!
- *Are You My Neighbor?*—Vegetables acting out the Good Samaritan story followed by a sci-fi spoof: Can two "oddball" crew members save the spaceship?
- *"God Wants Me to Forgive Them?!?"*—Will one sad asparagus forgive a bunch of cranky grapes? In the second part, first mate Larry isn't looking and crashes his boat on an uncharted island. The skipper and the passengers are upset.
- *"Where's God When I'm S-Scared?"*— Jr. Asparagus watches a scary movie and meets some new friends. Next, see Daniel deal with the lions.

Your mom or dad can order these videos. Tell them the form is on page 63, or they can call weekdays toll-free:

1-800-224-2735 (U.S.)
1-800-461-4114 (Canada)

Phone orders may be placed with a VISA, MasterCard, or Discover Card.